CONNECTICUT

EXPLORE THE UNITED STATES

Sarah

Big Buddy BOOKS

VISIT US AT
www.abdopublishing.com

Published by ABDO Publishing Company, PO Box 398166, Minneapolis, MN 55439.

Copyright © 2013 by Abdo Consulting Group, Inc. International copyrights reserved in all countries. No part of this book may be reproduced in any form without written permission from the publisher. Big Buddy Books™ is a trademark and logo of ABDO Publishing Company.

Printed in the United States of America, North Mankato, Minnesota.
022012
092012

PRINTED ON RECYCLED PAPER

Coordinating Series Editor: Rochelle Baltzer
Contributing Editors: BreAnn Rumsch, Marcia Zappa
Graphic Design: Adam Craven
Cover Photograph: *iStockphoto*: ©iStockphoto.com/hartfordphoto.
Interior Photographs/Illustrations: *AP Photo*: AP Photo (p. 25), Bob Child (pp. 26, 27), Jae C. Hong (p. 21), North Wind Picture Archives via AP Images (p. 13); *Getty Images*: FPG (p. 19), Hulton Archive (p. 23), Richard Messina/Hartford Courant/MCT via Getty Images (p. 19), Jack Rosen/Photo Researchers (p. 30); *Glow Images*: Superstock (p. 26); *iStockphoto*: ©iStockphoto.com/DenisTangneyJr (pp. 5, 11), ©iStockphoto.com/Joesboy (p. 30), ©iStockphoto.com/vmnphoto (p. 9); *Shutterstock*: Hung Chung Chih (p. 27), Arthur Connors (p. 11), Enfi (p. 29), Donald Gargano (p. 27), Jared Huckle (p. 9), Phillip Lange (p. 30), Laura Stone (pp. 17, 23), gregg williams (p. 30).

All population figures taken from the 2010 US census.

Library of Congress Cataloging-in-Publication Data

Tieck, Sarah, 1976-
  Connecticut / Sarah Tieck.
    p. cm. -- (Explore the United States)
  ISBN 978-1-61783-345-8
  1. Connecticut--Juvenile literature. I. Title.
  F94.3.T54 2012
  974.6--dc23
                          2012000758

Contents

ONE NATION

The United States is a **diverse** country. It has farmland, cities, coasts, and mountains. Its people come from many different backgrounds. And, its history covers more than 200 years.

Today, the country includes 50 states. Connecticut is one of these states. Let's learn more about this state and its story!

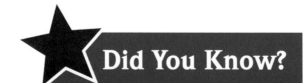

Did You Know?

Connecticut became a state on January 9, 1788. It was the fifth state to join the nation.

There are many lighthouses on Connecticut's coast.

5

CONNECTICUT UP CLOSE

The United States has four main **regions**. Connecticut is in the Northeast.

Connecticut has three states on its borders. New York is west. Massachusetts is north. And Rhode Island is east. The Long Island **Sound** is south.

Connecticut is a small state. It has a total area of 5,004 square miles (12,960 sq km). Still, about 3.6 million people live there.

Did You Know?

Washington DC is the US capital city. Puerto Rico is a US commonwealth. This means it is governed by its own people.

REGIONS OF THE UNITED STATES

Legend:
- □ = West
- ▨ = Midwest
- ▤ = South
- ▨ = Northeast

CANADA

WASHINGTON
MONTANA
OREGON
IDAHO
WYOMING
NEVADA
UTAH
CALIFORNIA
COLORADO
ARIZONA
NEW MEXICO

NORTH DAKOTA
MINNESOTA
SOUTH DAKOTA
WISCONSIN
NEBRASKA
IOWA
KANSAS
MISSOURI
OKLAHOMA
ARKANSAS
TEXAS
LOUISIANA

MICHIGAN
ILLINOIS
INDIANA
OHIO
KENTUCKY
TENNESSEE
MISSISSIPPI
ALABAMA
GEORGIA
FLORIDA

VERMONT
MAINE
NEW HAMPSHIRE
MASSACHUSETTS
NEW YORK
RHODE ISLAND
CONNECTICUT
PENNSYLVANIA
NEW JERSEY
Washington DC ★
DELAWARE
WEST VIRGINIA
MARYLAND
VIRGINIA
NORTH CAROLINA
SOUTH CAROLINA

PACIFIC OCEAN
ATLANTIC OCEAN
GULF OF MEXICO

ALASKA
MEXICO
HAWAII
PUERTO RICO

N
W E
S

7

IMPORTANT CITIES

Hartford is the **capital** of Connecticut. It is also the third-largest city in the state. It is home to 124,775 people. Hartford is sometimes called the "**Insurance City.**" That's because it has many insurance companies.

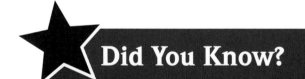

Did You Know?

The Hartford Courant was first printed in 1764. It is one of the oldest newspapers in the United States.

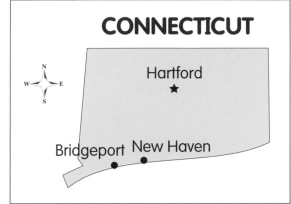

CONNECTICUT

Hartford

Bridgeport   New Haven

The state capitol is next to Bushnell Park. This was the first public park in the United States.

Hartford is located next to the Connecticut River.

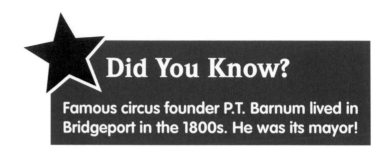
Bridgeport is Connecticut's largest city. It has 144,229 people. It is located on Long Island **Sound**. Many boats come and go from this city.

New Haven is the state's second-largest city. It has 129,779 people. It is home to Yale University. This is considered one of the country's best colleges.

Bridgeport is known for music and theater.

Yale is the third-oldest US college. It was founded in 1701.

11

CONNECTICUT IN HISTORY

Connecticut's history includes Native Americans and the beginning of the United States. Native Americans have lived in the area for hundreds of years.

People from England settled the land in the 1630s. The area became a colony. In 1775, colonists fought in the **Revolutionary War**. This led to the forming of the United States.

Men from Connecticut signed up to fight in the Revolutionary War.

Timeline

1633

The first English settlement in Connecticut was founded in Windsor.

1775

Colonists began fighting in the **Revolutionary War**.

1783

Connecticut native Noah Webster printed *The American Spelling Book*. Later, he printed an important American dictionary.

1600s

1700s

1776

American colonies signed the Declaration of Independence. This paper said America was ready to rule itself as a nation.

1788

Connecticut became the fifth state on January 9.

2011

More than two feet (0.6 m) of snow fell during an October storm. About 50,000 people in Connecticut lost power for more than a week.

1864

The first accident **insurance** in the United States was sold in Hartford.

1910

The US Coast Guard Academy moved to New London.

1800s

1900s

2000s

Hartford was named the only **capital** of Connecticut. It had been co-capital with New Haven since 1701.

Connecticut celebrated 200 years as a state.

1988

1875

15

ACROSS THE LAND

Connecticut has hills covered in forests. It also has beaches and harbors along the Long Island **Sound**. The Connecticut River flows through the center of the state and into the sound.

Many types of animals make their homes in this state. Some of these include deer, muskrats, and wild turkeys.

Did You Know?

The temperature in Connecticut changes with the seasons. In July, the average is 71°F (22°C). In January, it is 26°F (-3°C).

The Long Island Sound connects to the Atlantic Ocean.

EARNING A LIVING

Connecticut has many businesses. Some companies make products such as **chemicals** and **vehicle** parts. Others help people with money and **insurance** needs. Some people have jobs that help visitors to the state.

Connecticut is known for making clocks (*above*) and brass products (*right*). Some have been made there for hundreds of years.

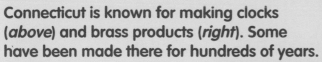

Sports Page

Many people think of college sports when they think of Connecticut. That's because the state is home to the University of Connecticut Huskies.

The Huskies are known for their basketball teams. The men's team won its third national championship in 2011. And, the women's team won its seventh in 2010!

Jim Calhoun has coached the Huskies men's basketball team since 1986.

Hometown Heroes

Many famous people have lived in Connecticut. Nathan Hale was born in Coventry in 1755.

Hale was an American soldier during the **Revolutionary War**. He became famous for saying, "I only regret that I have but one life to lose for my country." When he died in 1776, people remembered him as a hero.

People can still visit the Nathan Hale Homestead. It was built in 1776 by his family.

Hale was a spy for General George Washington during the Revolutionary War.

Charles Goodyear was born in New Haven in 1800. He discovered a **process** that made it possible to use rubber in new ways. This allowed rubber to be used to make shoes, hats, balls, and tires.

Famous author Mark Twain lived in Hartford from about 1871 to 1891. He wrote some of his most famous books while living there.

Goodyear is remembered as a famous inventor.

Twain wrote *The Adventures of Tom Sawyer* and *Adventures of Huckleberry Finn*.

25

Tour Book

Do you want to go to Connecticut? If you visit the state, here are some places to go and things to do!

★ Explore

Connecticut is known for its fall colors. It has more than 90 state parks and 30 state forests! Hike around Gillette Castle in Gillette Castle State Park.

★ Discover

Visit Dinosaur State Park near Hartford. There, you can see 200 million-year-old dinosaur tracks!

★ Eat

Try fresh seafood caught off the coast. If you don't like that, grab a burger at Louis' Lunch in New Haven. Many say the first hamburger was served there around 1900.

★ Play

Toss a Frisbee on Yale's campus. Some say students there made up this game around 1920. They tossed empty pie plates from the Frisbie Pie Company.

★ Learn

Mystic Seaport has an area built to look like an 1800s whaling village. Tour old buildings. And visit the last American wooden whaling ship, the *Charles W. Morgan*!

A GREAT STATE

The story of Connecticut is important to the United States. The people and places that make up this state offer something special to the country. Together with all the states, Connecticut helps make the United States great.

Wadsworth Falls is one of the state's beautiful sights.

Fast Facts

Date of Statehood:
January 9, 1788

Population (rank):
3,574,097
(29th most-populated state)

Total Area (rank):
5,004 square miles
(48th largest state)

Motto:
"Qui Transtulit Sustinet"
(He Who Transplanted Still
Sustains)

Nickname:
Nutmeg State,
Constitution State

State Capital:
Hartford

Flag:

Flower: Mountain Laurel

Postal Abbreviation:
CT

Tree: White Oak

Bird: American Robin

Important Words

capital a city where government leaders meet.

chemical (KEH-mih-kuhl) a substance that can cause reactions and changes.

diverse made up of things that are different from each other.

insurance a contract that promises to guard people against a loss of money if something happens to them or their property.

process a set of actions done to change something.

region a large part of a country that is different from other parts.

Revolutionary War a war fought between England and the North American colonies from 1775 to 1783.

sound a long passage of water that separates an island from the mainland.

vehicle something used for carrying persons or large objects. Some examples are cars, trucks, boats, and airplanes.

Web Sites

To learn more about Connecticut, visit ABDO Publishing Company online. Web sites about Connecticut are featured on our Book Links page. These links are routinely monitored and updated to provide the most current information available.

www.abdopublishing.com

Index